Encouragement

Matters

By

Jamie Lynn

Copyright © 2017 by Jamie Lynn

www.aaronpublishing.com

Printed in the United States of America

First Printing, June2017

ISBN: 978-0-9989385-1-6

Published by

Aaron Publishing

PO Box 1144

Shelbyville, TN 37162

Acknowledgements

I have to thank a few people for having my back this past year. I have met some incredible people due to social media. I want to dedicate this book to ALL of you.

Patrick Osman thank you for being an incredible man of God. Thank you for believing in me when sometimes I just wanted to lie in bed. You are such an inspiration to thousands of people. I'm blessed that God allowed our paths to cross.

Terrliski Davis my brotha from another mother. You know exactly what to say to me to set me straight. I don't always want to hear it but I take it in. Thank you for being my brother in Christ. Thank you for loving me in spite of my flaws.

Richard Rankin for blessing my socks off when I least expected it to happen in my life. We all have our part in the kingdom and you do your part well. Thank you for all that you have done.

Frank Sagasta your knowledge on the greats always impresses me. You are such an encouragement to me. Thank you for being you. Thank you for being a phone call away so we can inspire each other for the kingdom of God. Great things ahead Sir.

I love all of you. I would not and could not be the woman I am today without any of you giving me a good kick every now and then to stay on track.

Last but not least my beautiful daughters. Briana, Rylee, and Mariah you are the reason I get up and keep going every day. Leaving these books behind for you girls to have something to look back on is what it is all about. All three of you have greatness in you. I am excited to see how that flourishes. I love all three of you very much.

Table of Content

Bitter or Better

Bitterness will rot your bones. Take all the

bad things that have and will happen to you in life
and

use it to make you better.

When life hands you lemons (bitter)

make lemonade. (better)

Notes

_____

_____

_____

_____

_____

_____

_____

_____

_____

Love

You are so loved no matter what you have done or been
through in your life. God's love is different from man's
love.

Love is patient, love is kind. It does not envy, it does not boast, it is not proud. It does not dishonor others, it is not self-seeking, it is not easily angered, it keeps no record of wrongs. Love does not delight in evil but rejoices with the truth. It always protects, always trusts, always hopes, always perseveres. Love never fails

1 Corinthians 13:4-8 NIV

Notes

_____

_____

_____

_____

_____

_____

_____

_____

_____

_____

_____

Trust

Trust is one of the hardest things for people to do. Trust in God that he is who he says he is. If he brought you to it he will bring you through it.

For I know the plans I have for you," declares the LORD, "plans to prosper you and not to harm you, plans to give you hope and a future.

Jeremiah 29:11 NIV

Notes

_____

_____

_____

_____

_____

_____

_____

_____

_____

_____

Honesty

You have to look at yourself and be honest.

How did you get where you are today?

YOU'RE CHOICES

When we become honest with ourselves real

change begins to happen.

A faithful person will be richly blessed,
but one eager to get rich will not go unpunished.

Proverbs 28:20 NIV

Notes

_____

_____

_____

_____

_____

_____

_____

_____

_____

Integrity

Integrity is not what you do when everyone
is watching. Integrity is doing the right
thing when no one is looking. God rewards
outwardly when you have integrity.

Whoever walks in integrity walks securely,
but whoever takes crooked paths will be found out.

Proverbs 10:9 NIV

Notes

_____

_____

_____

_____

_____

_____

_____

_____

_____

_____

Hurt

Hurt in our lives is inevitable. Take your

hurt and use it to change other people's

lives. The hurt you feel right now is not for you

nor will it last forever. The pain is temporary.

I consider that our present sufferings are not worth comparing with the glory that will be revealed in us.

Romans 8:18 NIV

Notes

_____

_____

_____

_____

_____

_____

_____

_____

_____

_____

Heart Issues

Our heart is deceiving and wicked.

Things that come out of our mouth are from

Deep-rooted heart issues. Ask God to give you

a new heart. Flow in love.

Create in me a pure heart, O God,
and renew a steadfast spirit within me.

Psalm 51:10 NIV

Notes

_____

_____

_____

_____

_____

_____

_____

_____

_____

_____

Hold On

You are on the brink of giving up....

STOP

hold on because your blessing is

right around the corner.

Because he[a] loves me," says the LORD, "I will rescue him;
I will protect him, for he acknowledges my name.
He will call on me, and I will answer him;
I will be with him in trouble,
I will deliver him and honor him.
With long life I will satisfy him
and show him my salvation."

Psalm 91:14-16 NIV

Notes

_____

_____

_____

_____

_____

_____

_____

_____

_____

_____

Grass Is Not Greener

If it looks too good to be true

than it is. It takes hard work

in anything you do in life. Don't

make a quick decision because it looks good

at the moment. Do your

research before jumping two feet into

anything.

Notes

_____

_____

_____

_____

_____

_____

_____

_____

_____

_____

Relationships

God created us to have relationships. He knew that we

could not be alone. Value the people that come

and go in your life. Every relationship can teach

you something!!!

You did not choose me, but I chose you and appointed you so that you might go and bear fruit—fruit that will last—and so that whatever you ask in my name the Father will give you.

John 15:16 NIV

Notes

_____

_____

_____

_____

_____

_____

_____

_____

_____

_____

Forgiveness

Forgiveness is not an option. We are
commanded to forgive no matter what
the offense is in our lives. Forgiveness
is **NOT** saying what the person
did was ok. It's saying you are releasing
the offense to God so YOU can be set free.

You did not choose me, but I chose you and appointed you so that you might go and bear fruit—fruit that will last—and so that whatever you ask in my name the Father will give you.

Matthew 6:14-15 NIV

Notes

Distractions

In today's society it is easy to get distracted.

Be aware of people and things that

take you away from your destiny.

Make sure you write out a plan then

follow through.

Rise up; this matter is in your hands. We will support you, so take courage and do it."

Ezra 10:4

Notes

_____

_____

_____

_____

_____

_____

_____

_____

_____

_____

Fear of Failure

Fear of failure is an excuse to stay in

your comfort zone. Failure is a part of

being great. Get up stop making excuses

FACE THE FEAR!!!!

Have I not commanded you? Be strong and courageous. Do not be afraid; do not be discouraged, for the LORD your God will be with you wherever you go."

Joshua 1:9 NIV

Notes

_____

_____

_____

_____

_____

_____

_____

_____

_____

_____

Faith

We are only required to have

a mustard seed of faith.

Faith is what gets you through the

hardships in your life. Keep pushing

even though you can't see how

it will turn out.

For no word from God will ever fail."

Luke 1:37 NIV

Notes

_____

_____

_____

_____

_____

_____

_____

_____

_____

_____

Rejection Happens

You will get rejected in your life.

The good news about rejection, it positions

you for the direction God wants you to go.

Don't look at rejection as negativity.

Look at it as protection and set up.

As you come to him, the living Stone—rejected by humans but chosen by God and precious to him—

1Peter 2:4 NIV

Notes

_____

_____

_____

_____

_____

_____

_____

_____

_____

Give Thanks

People seem to be most thankful around the holidays.

Chose to be thankful every day.

Even in bad situations thank God for something

because he still has purpose for your life.

give thanks in all circumstances; for this is God's will for you in Christ Jesus.

1 Thessalonians 5:18 NIV

Notes

_____

_____

_____

_____

_____

_____

_____

_____

_____

_____

Cry it Out

There will be times in your life

you just have to cry it out. Crying is not

a sign of weakness. It shows people you

have a heart. Crying cleanses our soul.

Let it out!!!

In my distress I called to the LORD,
and he answered me.
From deep in the realm of the dead I called for help,
and you listened to my cry.

Jonah 2:2 NIV

Notes

_____

_____

_____

_____

_____

_____

_____

_____

_____

_____

Pray

Prayer changes things in your life.

Don't be ashamed to pray about everything

and everywhere. God loves when we

come to him in prayer.

Therefore confess your sins to each other and pray for each other so that you may be healed. The prayer of a righteous person is powerful and effective.

James 5:16 NIV

Notes

_____

_____

_____

_____

_____

_____

_____

_____

_____

_____

Laugh

Laughter is medicine to our soul.

Sometimes you just have to laugh when things

are not working out. Laughter is

contagious.

a time to weep and a time to laugh,

a time to mourn and a time to dance,

Ecclesiastes 3:4 NIV

Notes

_____

_____

_____

_____

_____

_____

_____

_____

_____

_____

Inner Struggles

We all have inner struggles. Just know you

have been given the strength and power

to overcome

depression, lack of peace, anxiety, fear, etc....

Do I bring to the moment of birth
and not give delivery?" says the LORD.
"Do I close up the womb
when I bring to delivery?" says your God.

Isaiah 66:9

Notes

_____

_____

_____

_____

_____

_____

_____

_____

_____

_____

Give Back

Giving back is the most rewarding feeling

a human can experience.

Giving back gives people joy and a sense

of accomplishment.

Giving is not just money!!

Give, and it will be given to you. A good measure, pressed down, shaken together and running over, will be poured into your lap. For with the measure you use, it will be measured to you."

Luke 6:38 NIV

Notes

_____

_____

_____

_____

_____

_____

_____

_____

_____

_____

Death of a Loved One

It's never easy to deal with the losing

someone you love to death.

Give yourself time to grieve. Understand

you never get over them being gone.

You just learn how to deal with them in your heart.

The LORD is close to the brokenhearted
and saves those who are crushed in spirit.

Psalm 34:18 NIV

Notes

_____

_____

_____

_____

_____

_____

_____

_____

_____

_____

Single Life

Being single is a blessing.

It allows you to focus on God more.

Be ok with hanging out with YOU.

Being single is not negative.

Embrace it!!

Singleness is a wonderful gift!!!

Notes

_____

_____

_____

_____

_____

_____

_____

_____

_____

_____

Marriage

Marriage is a beautiful union between husbands

and wives. It allows two to become one and be

fruitful.

You both will do things imperfect.

Remember to always put the other person first

and forgive their imperfections.

Chose love daily.

So they are no longer two, but one flesh. Therefore what God has joined together, let no one separate."

Matthew 19:6 NIV

Notes

_____

_____

_____

_____

_____

_____

_____

_____

_____

_____

God's Grace

We sometimes get into slumps over

our mistakes.

We feel like we are not good enough for

God.

God's grace allows us to do it over again with a

clean slate.

God's grace is bigger than our mistake.

The law was brought in so that the trespass might increase. But where sin increased, grace increased all the more,

Romans 5:20 NIV

Notes

_____

_____

_____

_____

_____

_____

_____

_____

_____

_____

Anger

Anger is very hurtful and solves nothing.

When you say or do something in anger it can be

forgiven but not forgotten.

We all have limits but be wise to not make yourself

look foolish in the heat of the MOMENT!!

*In your anger do not sin [a]: Do not let the sun go down while you are still angry, and
do not give the devil a foothold.*

Ephesians 4:26-27 NIV

Notes

_____

_____

_____

_____

_____

_____

_____

_____

_____

_____

Health

Our body is a temple. Chose to eat good foods, drink plenty of water, rest, exercise, and think positive. You will have great results, reduce disease, and sickness.

The LORD sustains them on their sickbed and restores them from their bed of illness.

Psalms 41:3

Notes

_____

_____

_____

_____

_____

_____

_____

_____

_____

_____

Money

Money is not the root of all evil. It's how we

manage it.

God promises to prosper us but we have

to be good stewards over the little.

His master replied, 'Well done, good and faithful servant! You have been faithful with a few things; I will put you in charge of many things. Come and share your master's happiness!'

Matthew 25:23 NIV

Notes

_____

_____

_____

_____

_____

_____

_____

_____

_____

_____

Gifts

Discover the gift God has given you.

We all have something that comes natural to us.

People are waiting for you so they can be

set free and go to heaven.

WHAT ARE YOU WAITING FOR????

Every good and perfect gift is from above, coming down from the Father of the heavenly lights, who does not change like shifting shadows.

James 1:17 NIV

Notes

Surrender

Surrender everything to God so he can give you

ALL he has for you.

You will know when you have surrendered all

to HIM because you

will have peace that surpasses all understanding

in the midst of the storm that is around you.

but those who hope in the LORD
will renew their strength.
They will soar on wings like eagles;
they will run and not grow weary,
they will walk and not be faint

Isaiah 40:31 NIV

Notes

_____

_____

_____

_____

_____

_____

_____

_____

_____

_____

_____

Success

Success is walking in your gifts and talents

with excellence.

When you do this the money will be

sure to follow.

Be successful at knowing and be the wonderful

person you are.

Commit to the LORD whatever you do,
and he will establish your plans.

Proverbs 16:3 NIV

Notes

_____

_____

_____

_____

_____

_____

_____

_____

_____

_____

Final Encouragement

Thank you for investing in this small book of encouragement. My

prayer for you is to use this book when you are having a bad day.

Be encouraged when you are going through trials. We all go through

things but praise God we have hope in HIM.

Father in the name of Jesus I pray for every reader to walk away feeling inspired and encouraged in whatever is going on in their life. Thank you for the person reading this right now. Let them know and realize that you have great things in store for them. Trust in God he has got this and you. Amen.

Notes

_____

_____

_____

_____

_____

_____

_____

_____

_____

_____

www.ingramcontent.com/pod-product-compliance
Lightning Source LLC
Chambersburg PA
CBHW071424040426
42445CB00012BA/1283